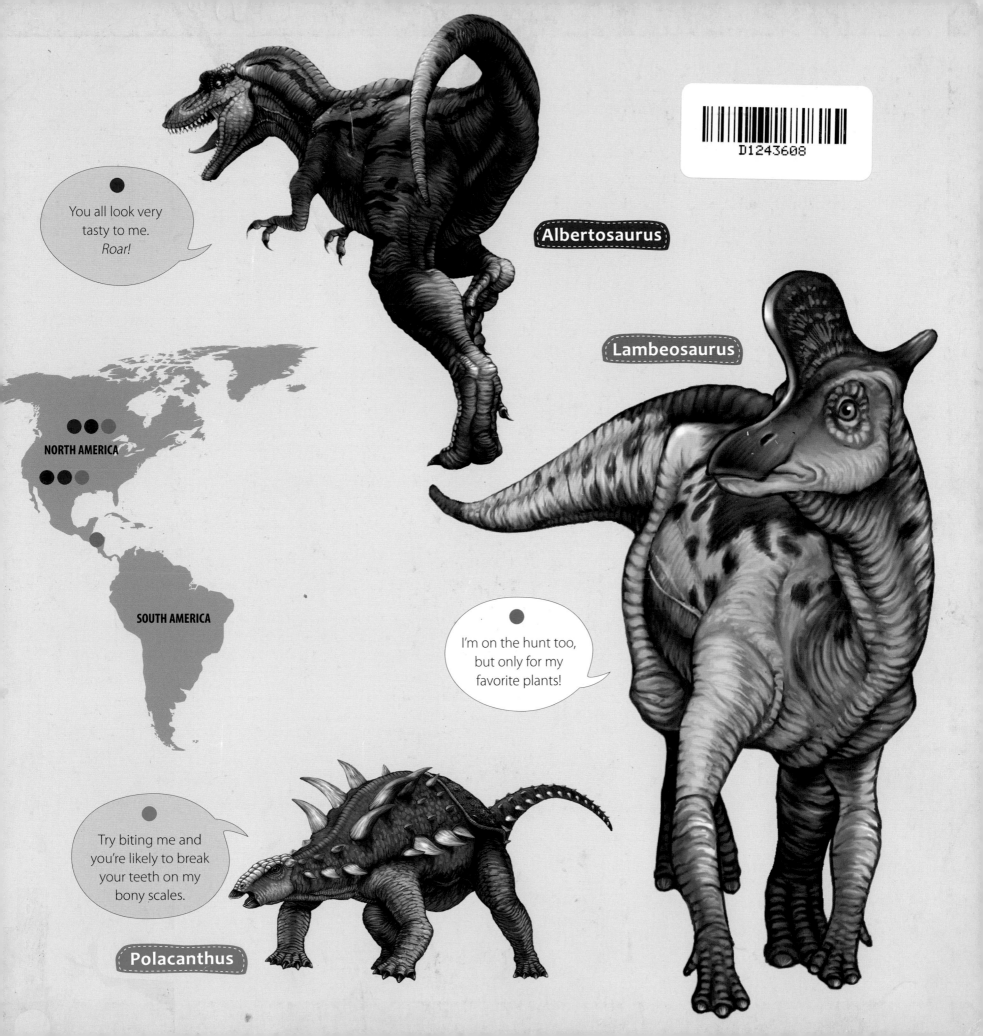

big & SMALL

Original Korean text and illustrations by Dreaming Tortoise
Korean edition © Aram Publishing

This English edition published by big & SMALL in 2016
by arrangement with Aram Publishing
English text edited by Scott Forbes
English edition © big & SMALL 2016

Distributed in the United States and Canada by
Lerner Publishing Group, Inc.
241 First Avenue North
Minneapolis, MN 55401 U. S. A.
www.lernerbooks.com

Photo credits:
Page 28, top: © Claire Houck
Page 29, top: © Sebastian Bergmann; middle © J.W Hulke

To learn more about dinosaur fossils, see page 28.
For information on the main groups of dinosaurs,
see the Dinosaur Family Tree on page 30.

Fearsome
Albertosaurus

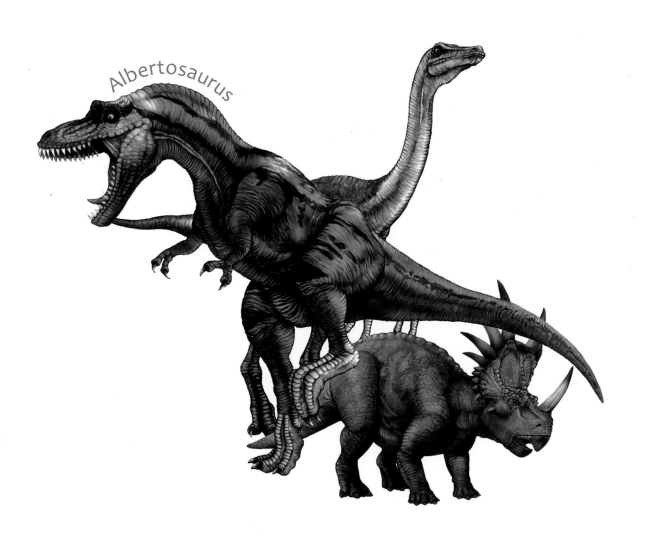

Albertosaurus

big & SMALL

Styracosaurus

SAY IT:
Sty-rah-co-SAW-rus

A young Styracosaurus and its mother were in a forest clearing, chewing quietly on some delicious leaves. The mother heard rustling in the bushes. She turned toward the sound.

Coming toward them was a Daspletosaurus, a fearsome meat-eater. It took one look at the Styracosaurus's scary horns and decided that perhaps it wasn't so hungry after all.
Then it turned and crept away.

Styracosaurus means "long-spiked lizard." This big, bulky dinosaur had long horns on its neck frill and a huge horn on its nose. These weapons made it difficult for other dinosaurs to attack it.

Nearby, two young Styracosaurus were playing. They pushed and shoved each other, and raced back and forth between the trees.

Their mother kept a close watch on them and signaled to them not to go too far away. She was always looking out for meat-eating dinosaurs that might attack her young.

LENGTH: 18 feet (5.5 meters)

HEIGHT: 8.5 feet (2.6 meters)

WEIGHT: 3.3 tons (3 tonnes)

WHEN IT LIVED: TRIASSIC JURASSIC CRETACEOUS

GROUP: Ceratopsians

DIET: Plants

WHERE IT LIVED: North America (USA, Canada)

Young male Styracosaurus often used their horns in play fights. Sometimes they fought to show their strength and win the attention of a female.

An Alectrosaurus had just caught a Prenocephale and was preparing to feed on it. Suddenly a huge Tarbosaurus appeared out of nowhere.

10

PRENOCEPHALE

GROUP: Pachycephalosaurs
DIET: Plants
WHEN IT LIVED: Late Cretaceous
WHERE IT LIVED: Asia (Mongolia)
LENGTH: 6.6 feet (2 meters)
HEIGHT: 3.3 feet (1 meter)
WEIGHT: 77 pounds
(35 kilograms)

TARBOSAURUS

GROUP: Theropods
DIET: Meat
WHEN IT LIVED: Late Cretaceous
WHERE IT LIVED: Asia (Mongolia, China)
LENGTH: 40–43 feet (12–13 meters)
HEIGHT: 16.5 feet (5 meters)
WEIGHT: 6.6–7.7 tons
(6–7 tonnes)

Alectrosaurus growled, but quickly backed off.
It was no match for Tarbosaurus, so it
left its prey for the bigger dinosaur.

The Alectroasurus wandered off across the dry plains.
All at once a pair of Bactrosaurus rushed past.
They were gasping for breath, and had clearly been
running away from another hunter.
A Bactrosaurus was easy prey for the Alectroasurus,
and it quickly seized one in its claws.

LENGTH: 16.5 feet
(5 meters)

HEIGHT: 6 feet
(1.8 meters)

WEIGHT: 0.5 tons
(0.45 tonnes)

WHEN IT LIVED: **TRIASSIC** | **JURASSIC** | **CRETACEOUS**

GROUP: **Theropods**

DIET: **Meat**

WHERE IT LIVED:
Asia (China)

Alectroasurus was a distant relative of Tyrannosaurus. Even though it was much smaller than its giant cousin, it was almost as ferocious.

Like Tyrannosaurus, Alectroasurus had strong legs for running fast, and powerful jaws and sharp teeth to grab and tear apart its prey.

BACTROSAURUS

GROUP: Ornithopods
DIET: Plants
WHEN IT LIVED: Late Cretaceous
WHERE IT LIVED: Asia (China)
LENGTH: 20 feet (6 meters)
HEIGHT: 6.6 feet (2 meters)
WEIGHT: 1.1–1.7 tons
(1–1.5 tonnes)

13

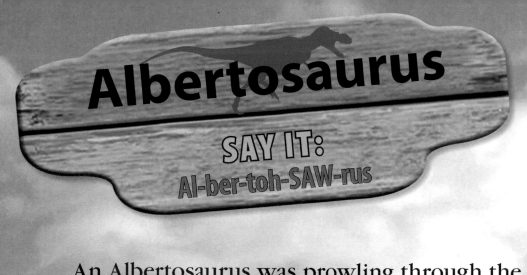

Albertosaurus

SAY IT:
Al-ber-toh-SAW-rus

An Albertosaurus was prowling through the forest, looking for food. In a clearing, it came upon a Pentaceratops and her baby.

The Albertosaurus tried to snatch up the baby Pentaceratops, but its mother kept blocking the huge meat-eater, forcing it back with her horns.

PENTACERATOPS

GROUP: Ceratopsians
DIET: Plants
WHEN IT LIVED: Late Cretaceous
WHERE IT LIVED: North America
(USA, Canada)
LENGTH: 16.5–26 feet (5–8 meters)
HEIGHT: 8 feet (2.5 meters)
WEIGHT: 5.5 tons
(5 tonnes)

HEIGHT: **13 feet**
(**4 meters**)

WEIGHT: **1.6 tons**
(**1.5 tonnes**)

LENGTH: **30 feet**
(**9 meters**)

WHEN IT LIVED: | TRIASSIC | JURASSIC | CRETACEOUS

GROUP: **Theropods**

DIET: **Meat**

WHERE IT LIVED:
North America
(Canada, USA)

15

The baby Pentaceratops scuttled away,
into the safety of some nearby bushes.
Its mother held off her attacker, but
then another Albertosaurus arrived.
She was no match for two big meat-eaters,
and soon they had her pinned to the ground.

16

Albertosaurus was a fierce and clever hunter. Its massive jaws contained about 60 long, sharp teeth and it could run fast over short distances. Often, two or more Albertosaurus would work together to trap prey.

Gallimimus

SAY IT:
Gal-lee-MY-mus

TSINTAOSAURUS

GROUP: Ornithopods
DIET: Meat
WHEN IT LIVED: Late Cretaceous
WHERE IT LIVED: Asia (China, Korea)
LENGTH: 30–33 feet (9–10 meters)
HEIGHT: 13 feet (4 meters)
WEIGHT: 3.3–4.4 tons
(3–4 tonnes)

The Gallimimus was starving.
It hadn't managed to catch
anything all morning.
It went to the river to take a drink.
Bending down to the water, it spotted
a little lizard crawling across a rock.
In an instant, the Gallimimus whipped
its long neck around and snapped up
the lizard. Food at last!

Gallimimus means "chicken-like dinosaur." But this dinosaur looked more like an ostrich than a chicken.

Gallimimus was a fast dinosaur. It could run at the speed of a car driving on a freeway! It usually ate insects and small reptiles, but would sometimes eat fruit too.

For a dinosaur, Gallimimus had a large brain. So it was probably one of the smarter dinosaurs.

LENGTH: 16.5–20 feet (5–6 meters)

HEIGHT: 6.5–7.5 feet (2–2.3 meters)

WEIGHT: 350–485 pounds (160–220 kilograms)

WHEN IT LIVED: TRIASSIC | JURASSIC | CRETACEOUS

GROUP: Theropods

DIET: Meat

WHERE IT LIVED: Asia (China, Mongolia)

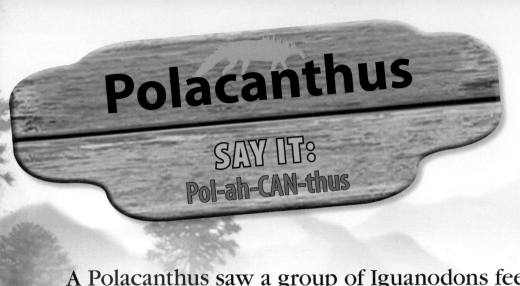

Polacanthus

A Polacanthus saw a group of Iguanodons feeding on trees and shrubs. It walked up beside the tall, gentle Iguanodons and started eating too. It knew that the Iguanodons were likely to spot any attackers before it did. If the Iguanodons started running, the Polacanthus would do the same.

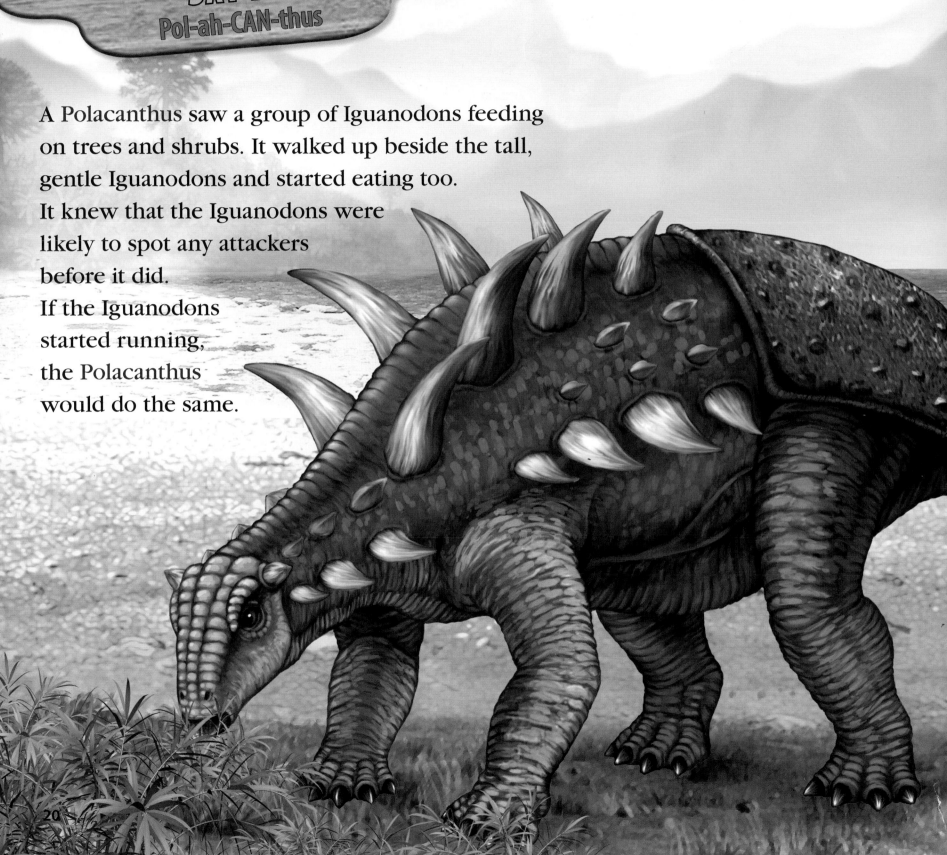

The Iguanodons didn't mind the Polacanthus feeding with them. Polacanthus only ate leaves near the ground, while they could easily reach leaves higher up in the trees.
So they weren't competing with each other for food.

IGUANODON

GROUP: Ornithopods
DIET: Plants
WHEN IT LIVED: Early Cretaceous
WHERE IT LIVED: North America (USA),
Asia (Mongolia), Europe (UK, Germany),
Africa (Tunisia)
LENGTH: 20–36 feet (6–11 meters)
HEIGHT: 16.5 feet (5 meters)
WEIGHT: 3.3–6.6 tons
(3–6 tonnes)

LENGTH: **16.5 feet** (5 meters)	HEIGHT: **5 feet** (1.5 meters)	WEIGHT: **0.9 tons** (0.8 tonnes)

WHEN IT LIVED:	TRIASSIC	JURASSIC	CRETACEOUS

GROUP: **Ankylosaurs**	DIET: **Plants**

WHERE IT LIVED:
Europe
(UK)

Suddenly the Iguanodons sensed danger and ran off.
The Polacanthus scurried toward some bushes to hide.
But before it got there, a pair of Neovenators appeared.
The Polacanthus swung its tail at its attackers.
It knew it couldn't run away, so it dropped to
the ground and lay flat on its stomach.

NEOVENATOR

GROUP: Theropods
DIET: Meat
WHEN IT LIVED: Early Cretaceous
WHERE IT LIVED: Europe (UK)
LENGTH: 26 feet (8 meters)
HEIGHT: 8 feet (2.5 meters)
WEIGHT: 0.8 tons
(0.75 tonnes)

Polacanthus's back was covered in armor-like plates and bony, pointed horns that looked like big thorns — Polacanthus means "many thorns."

When attacked, Polacanthus lay on the ground to protect its soft belly. Attackers found it hard to bite through its plates and horns, and often gave up in frustration.

Lambeosaurus

SAY IT:
Lam-bee-oh-SAW-rus

GORGOSAURUS

GROUP: Theropods
DIET: Meat
WHEN IT LIVED: Late Cretaceous
WHERE IT LIVED: North America
(USA, Canada)
LENGTH: 26 feet (8 meters)
HEIGHT: 8 feet (2.5 meters)
WEIGHT: 2.8 tons
(2.5 tonnes)

A Lambeosaurus made a loud hooting noise to warn others in its group — a Gorgosaurus was charging toward them! At once, the whole herd of Lambeosaurus began to run. Babies followed their mothers. None of them looked back. They ran as fast as they could.

Lambeosaurus made a hooting sound by blowing air through tubes that ran from its mouth and nose up through its crest.

25

The Lambeosaurus halted at the edge of a lake.
At first all seemed quiet, but then they heard the growling
of another dangerous hunter, Appalachiosaurus.
It wasn't safe here either. So they raised the alarm
once more, and sped away.

Lambeosaurus was a large plant-eater. That meant small meat-eaters would not usually attack it.
But if a larger hunter attacked, Lambeosaurus had only one way to protect itself — run away, fast!

APPALACHIOSAURUS

GROUP: Theropods
DIET: Meat
WHEN IT LIVED: Late Cretaceous
WHERE IT LIVED: North America (USA)
LENGTH: 23 feet (7 meters)
HEIGHT: 8 feet (2.5 meters)
WEIGHT: 0.7 tons
(0.65 tonnes)

LENGTH: 30–50 feet
(9–15 meters)

HEIGHT: 30 feet
(9 meters)

WEIGHT: 3.3–9.4 tons
(3–8.5 tonnes)

WHEN IT LIVED:	TRIASSIC	JURASSIC	CRETACEOUS

GROUP: **Ornithopods** DIET: **Plants**

WHERE IT LIVED:
North America
(Canada, USA, Mexico)

Dinosaur Fossils

Fossils are the remains of dinosaurs. They can be hard parts of dinosaurs, such as bones and teeth, that have slowly turned to stone. Or they may be impressions of bones, teeth, or skin preserved in rocks.

▶ Model of Styracosaurus skull

 ## Styracosaurus

US dinosaur hunter Charles Sternberg discovered the first fossils of Styracosaurus in what is now Dinosaur Provincial Park, in the province of Alberta in Canada, in 1912. Canadian expert Lawrence Lambe studied the fossils and gave the dinosaur its name. Since then, Styracosaurus fossils have been found in many parts of western Canada and the western USA.

 ## Alectrosaurus

In 1923, a group of dinosaur hunters from the American Museum of Natural History in New York traveled to the Gobi Desert in Mongolia, Asia. There they discovered a number of new dinosaurs, including Alectrosaurus. The first Alectrosaurus fossil the explorers found was a nearly complete back leg. Next they found fossils of feet, claws and parts of the backbone. The American team took the fossils back to their museum. Since then scientists have studied the fossils closely and discovered that Alectrosaurus is related to Tyrannosaurus.

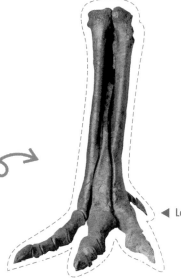

◀ Leg bone of Alectrosaurus

▲ Model of Gallimimus skeleton

Gallimimus

The first fossils of Gallimimus were discovered in Mongolia's Gobi Desert in 1963 by a team of Polish and Mongolian scientists led by Zofia Kielan-Jaworowska. But the dinosaur was not named until 1972. Since then a number of other bones and skeletons have been found, including bones of young Gallimimus.

▲ Model of Albertosaurus skeleton

Albertosaurus

Albertosaurus is named after the province of Alberta in Canada, where fossils of this dinosaur were first found, in 1884. The fossils were taken to New York, where a famous dinosaur expert called Henry Osborn studied them and gave the dinosaur its name. In 1910, dinosaur hunter Barnum Brown found many more Albertosaurus fossils at the Red Deer River in Alberta. Since then, about 1000 more Albertosaurus fossils have been discovered.

Polacanthus

In 1865, the Reverend William Fox found the first Polacanthus fossil on the Isle of Wight, off the south coast of England. It was only a small fossil and didn't tell scientists much. It wasn't until 1979 that Dr. William Blows discovered larger Polacanthus fossils that painted a clearer picture of this dinosaur.

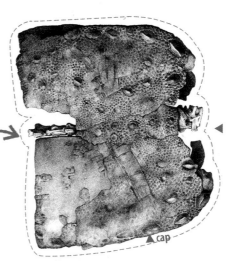
◄ Fossil of Polacanthus back plate

▲ cap

▶ Model of Lambeosaurus skeleton

Lambeosaurus

In 1923, Dr. William Parks discovered the first Lambeosaurus fossil in Alberta, Canada. He named the dinosaur after an earlier Canadian dinosaur expert called Lawrence Lambe. Rocks imprinted with the skin pattern of Lambeosaurus were also found. From those, we know that the dinosaur's skin was covered in hexagonal (six-sided) bumps.

THE DINOSAUR FAMILY TREE

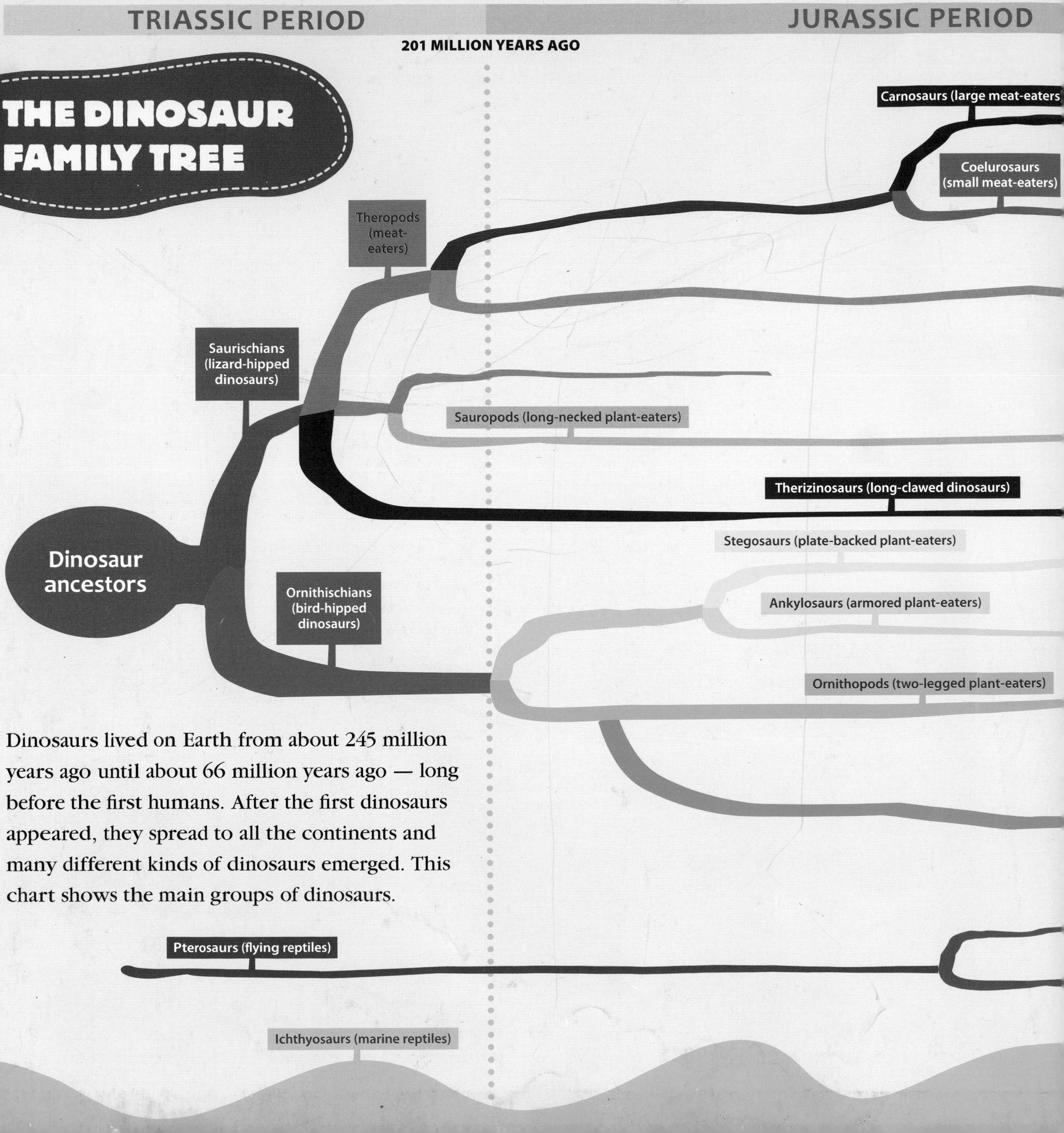

TRIASSIC PERIOD
JURASSIC PERIOD
201 MILLION YEARS AGO
Carnosaurs (large meat-eaters
Coelurosaurs (small meat-eaters)
Theropods (meat-eaters)
Saurischians (lizard-hipped dinosaurs)
Sauropods (long-necked plant-eaters)
Therizinosaurs (long-clawed dinosaurs)
Dinosaur ancestors
Stegosaurs (plate-backed plant-eaters)
Ankylosaurs (armored plant-eaters)
Ornithischians (bird-hipped dinosaurs)
Ornithopods (two-legged plant-eaters)
Pterosaurs (flying reptiles)
Ichthyosaurs (marine reptiles)

Dinosaurs lived on Earth from about 245 million years ago until about 66 million years ago — long before the first humans. After the first dinosaurs appeared, they spread to all the continents and many different kinds of dinosaurs emerged. This chart shows the main groups of dinosaurs.